LITTLE KNOWN STORIES

ALSO BY ERIC MILLER

Hula Girls

LITTLE KNOWN STORIES

Prose in Format

eric b. miller

Milbrown Press

© 2022 by Eric B. Miller

All rights reserved. No part of this book may be reproduced in any form or by any electronic or mechanical means, including information storage and retrieval systems, without written permission from the publisher, except by a reviewer who may quote passages in a review.

Cover photographs by Eric M. Miller
Author photo by Larry J. Cohen

Published by Milbrown Press
An imprint of JBM Publishing Company
1265 South Columbine Street
Denver, CO 80210
(303) 503-1739

Printed in the United States of America

ISBN: 979-8-9859113-0-5 (paperback)
ISBN: 979-8-9859113-1-2 (ebook)

Publisher's Cataloging-In-Publication Data
(Prepared by The Donohue Group, Inc.)

Names: Miller, Eric B., 1948– author.
Title: Little known stories : prose in format / Eric B. Miller.
Description: Denver, CO : Milbrown Press, [2022]
Identifiers: ISBN 9798985911305 (paperback) | ISBN 9798985911312 (ebook)
Subjects: LCSH: Miller, Eric B., 1948– —Marriage. | Terminally ill—Family relationships. | Wives—Death—Psychological aspects. | Assisted suicide—Psychological aspects. | Loss (Psychology) | LCGFT: Autobiographies. | Poetry. | Creative nonfiction.
Classification: LCC PS3613.I5361 Z46 2022 (print) | LCC PS3613.I5361 (ebook) | DDC 813/.6—dc23

Cover and page design by Pratt Brothers Composition

To those living out bad circumstances together

and to those enduring alone.

ACKNOWLEDGMENTS

My thanks to Dan and Jim Pratt of Pratt Brothers Composition for their sensitive work in cover design, text design, and editorial suggestions.

And to my brother Jeff for his close attention to every production aspect of this book as well as for his wise counsel on its content.

I make no reference in the book to the passage of Bill 1504 by the New Jersey state legislature in early 2019, or to our cruel and grueling six-month quest to make use of it, because I saw no need at the time of writing.

So I acknowledge here the sincere and caring individuals who fought for the bill on behalf of the tired and suffering who, like my wife, would want to leave while they still know themselves, while they can freely chose, and while they still try to love life.

My thanks to advocates in Oregon for their consultations and advice, and I extend my deepest gratitude to Dr. Deborah Pasik, one of many compassionate physicians, but the only one who stood up.

AUTHOR'S NOTE

Lisa and I were together for forty-one years. In her last year I saw most clearly the strength of her character, and particularly her instinct to create and build. I watched her meet every adversity by learning something or by making something. That is one of the things I learned from her, and this book is what I made.

ebm 2022

LITTLE KNOWN STORIES

1

In my dreams at night
you always come back to life.
Sometimes I find you sitting among the dead
on a gray beach
or sometimes you find me
looking for you there,
and we know each other
even at a distance.

It doesn't matter that you're dead.
It's just one of those little things
two people might notice about each other
after being apart,
and for the time
that a dream displaces reality
I don't wonder
how we came to be dreaming
in this strange place together.

2

The little rainbow
still comes through the window every sunny day
and lands in the same place on the floor.
She would slip her bare foot under it,
and balancing on the other leg,
bring the foot up
and slide the little rainbow
off her big toe
into the palm of her hand.
Then she would laugh.

I thought she could do anything.
If she is still here
her arms must be around me now
trying.

3

The difference between divorce and death
is a closet full of clothes.
Half of everything is still here
with the other half.
Except me.

4   IT TAKES A VILLAGE

She found out as a child
how many people
she couldn't count on.

But the library was there
so she went
and made herself
out of books.

5

I don't go looking for photographs of you.
They pass by
on screen saver
when I think too long or walk away.

At random
among slides of art projects in progress,
plaster molds and numbered pieces
on the basement floor,
clay maquettes on metal stands
and fabric on dress forms,

a picture of you comes up
looking right at the camera
with one of those funny little expressions
that lived a moment on your face
before you became ashes.

6

She couldn't sing
and wouldn't try in front of me.
But I put my ear to the floor every so often
when I heard a creaky little noise in the basement,
and there it was, singing,
soft, but there
like a baby crying in the back row of a church service.

The only sounds that come from down there now
are the grumblings of the old hot water heater,
the new furnace clicking on and off,
and the creaking lamentations
of an old house holding its own,
out of time and a little off-key some nights.

7

I would try
living one day at time
if days really passed that way
but I run day into night
night into day
from one thing to another
staying ahead
of thoughts of you
that catch up
and pass the baton
and the race is back on

and all this weary business
of counting hours
but never coming home to you
waking and sleeping without you
all the time between.

8

Hope,
that thing with feathers
I wear in public—
a little preposterous, a little outlandish,
like those hats
they put on Queen Elizabeth.

9

The only remaining word
of my old language
is the word babba-sigh.
Then I was taught to say butterfly
and I learned
what a butterfly is.

Babba-sighs and butterflies may have
coexisted for a while in the world,
but time finally buried the babba-sigh,
and now it is beyond recall
what I saw when I pointed
and exclaimed babba-sigh!

I am afraid
what happened to the babba-sighs
will happen to you,
if I let any more time go by.

10

Got up a few hours
before she would have,
made a breakfast
she would have liked,
made the bed
the way she showed me,
went food shopping
where she used to go.
Did some laundry
without arguing with her over it,
did some work in the garage
that would have pleased her,
made a four-course dinner
that would have surprised her,
worked at my desk a few hours
without her interruptions.
And then I went to bed,
figuring I did enough
heart-breaking things
for one day.

11

With so many of the living around,
looking like they don't know what to do with each other,
I wish I could want one of them
for myself
more than I want the one
who did not make it
to the party.
She expresses her regrets.

12

A stone
will not stand in the grass
for you,
nor will a tree
grow in your place.
I took you down to the ocean
and let you go in a tide rushing out,
free of the earth
that was so hard on you.

13

I sit on the front porch
looking at the trees,
watching birds flit through the canopy.

I smoke, drink tea
and think a long time
as if something could be done,
as if there were a way to apologize,
a way to make it up to you
talk it over
set things right
try again, start over
or go back and change what happened,
and then my mind is
shooting through the trees in all directions
like the birds.

14

My mother used to say,
"You two are so—"
Then, with words failing her,
she would bring her hands together
as if she were packing a snowball.
Not wanting to be too critical,
she would leave it at that.

As visual aids go,
it was not far off the mark.
As far as anyone knew,
you were guarded and reserved, not best described by
warm, generous, loving.
But everything you were not to them
you were to me.
I became like you,
you became like me,
and that way
we never slipped through each other's fingers.

15

After you died that night
I lay down beside you
and talked to you,
kissed you and held you
for a few hours
into the next day.

It felt like the beginning
of a bad time,
but I had no idea.

When I got up
to make the phone call about you,
I could have told the lady
there are
two
dead people here.

16

I could tell the day was coming.
But whenever she winced and she knew I saw it,
she looked up smiling.

This time
she peered at me over her eyeglasses and books
and the papers in her lap
to tell me her last day would be Sunday.

Then she went back
to figuring out a problem she had
drawing in perspective.

It looked like it was going to take a lot of work
and concentration,
now that she only had
till Sunday.

17

The only survivor
assesses his wounds
and considers the situation.

Mountains all around, snow
and trackless forest.
Who will find me here
so far off course?

Others have made it out
on foot
by themselves,
but surviving a crash is one thing,
starting a journey is another.
So I will stay with the wreckage.

Maybe tomorrow
I'll feel like shouting and waving my arms
frantically
at any glint of plane.

18

I don't have to worry anymore
about chest pains,
shortness of breath,
symptoms of any kind
that I would have to tell her about,
or, for that matter,
falling off the ladder.

Since she isn't here,
I won't be leaving her alone,
I'll just be leaving.

My Belgian grandmother would have said
"Tant pis."

19

What do you do
when you discover
that the most pyrrhic of victories
is living to fight another day?

What do you do then?

20

PART ONE

A few days before she died,
she sat in her chair in the kitchen
doing geometry on a chalk board
and told me
I could have a good life.

She had finished teaching me
all I needed to know,
and I had taken plenty of notes.

It was a natural mistake
for her to make,
thinking I could have a good life.
There was nothing wrong with me then.

PART TWO: FOR SD

As far as the good life I was supposed to have,
I let myself believe it once.

Foolish expectations
dug a big hole.
I climbed in
and folly was more than happy
to cover me over.

21

In fair Verona
where we lay our scene—
when we were young
and broke forth to civil strife and new mutiny,
she strode straight and tall
through the shouting and clamor
and grasped my flailing arms
in a grip I thought could break bones,
fixed my wild eyes
in hers and said fiercely
between her teeth
"Stop it!"
and she would not let go of me
until I understood
we were meant for each other.

22

I'm glad to see the lilies of the valley are gone
and I don't have to imagine any longer
reproach coming from the green leaves and white bells
gathered at the base of the big pine and bed of hostas.

They were used to coming inside this time of year
by the basket full and sitting in little vases
in every room of the house,
sending forth their delicate scent
and delighting her for days.

My mother showed her how to pull the stalk
neatly out of the leaves, tugging gently with two fingers,
the way she did in Belgium before the war
when she still believed in God.

So I left the lilies of the valley alone this year
to share their scent between themselves
and put each other to sleep
with stories of those
who once picked them.

23

In as much as her attentions
were diverted all her life
into fret, care and worry,
had she known then
what she found out later,
that she would die here
in our house,
in our bed and in my arms,
she would have rushed to fill
that newly made space in her mind
with fearlessness.

24

I saw the determination
in everything you did.
I saw the hard set of your face
when you looked over financial reports,
cooked, measured, calculated,
made things,
or stopped whatever you were doing
to listen to me finding
as many ways as there were
to hurt you.

I'm so sorry.
I would never do it again.

25

Some husbands
get a blanket thrown over them
where they lie.
I will go to sleep believing
my wife will wake me up gently
and say softly
come to bed now.

26

She made everything she did
look like what she did best,
except drawing.
Her father tried to teach her,
and numerous others,
but she gave up on drawing
and held the belief for many years
that she never could.

She took it up again
in her last year,
maybe because it seemed to be
a project worthy
of finishing her off.

So she read many books
bought drawing sets, charcoal,
sketch pads and paper,
put up blackboards,
constructed picture plane and
perspective devices
and suddenly
drawings were flying all over the place.

For a while it looked like
she was really getting somewhere.

27

I had ten years on her,
but mystique has an illusive dimensionality
that the math does not continue to support
for very long,
and once in a while
she would stop and look at me funny,
as if she had just caught a mistake
and discovered how small
the numbers were getting.

But maybe she knew all along,
and loving me might have been
one of those dubious conclusions
she never changed her mind about.

Knowing that part of her well,
I can say with assurance
that now that she has eternity
to mull over the infinite,
ten years would not do much
for me anyway.

28

No one would believe it
but we had a lot of fun that year
with little things
that were just between us.

It is harder to say something about fun
and being silly
than to tread out sorrow and loss
because fun and silly takes two,
and in this case some of it
had to do with intimacy and aging.

What I can say is
the neighbors may have heard a lot of laughing
through the bedroom window.

29

We bought three new sets of bed sheets.
She liked the blue ones.
The whites reminded her a little too much of the hospital,
and she died in the grays, which I tell them
wasn't their fault, just the luck of the draw
since we changed the sheets every time
she woke up drenched in sweat.

I don't know how long
I slept in the grays after her,
for I was in such glad mysterious wonder
that they still pulled to her side of the bed,
and I remember
how annoying that used to be
when she was here.

30 FAMOUS PEOPLE SHE WAS LIKE

To every cat who ever lived here
she was Mother Teresa.
They puddled in her lap by day
and slept on her at night.

To every dog
she was Queen Victoria
of all that went on in the house,
and Bismark of the yard.

31

The best one I drew depicted
Little Monkey and Big Monkey
on ladders, with wrenches,
taking the hands off a wall clock.

Next panel showed the Monkeys carrying the clock hands
(as long as the Monkeys were tall)
over their shoulders, like
Laurel and Hardy.

Last panel had Little Monkey up on the ladder
affixing a clock hand (with wrench)
to a giant armature of a heroic sculpture in progress,
with Big Monkey below,
holding the ladder and the other hand of the clock.

The clock hands, ladders and wrenches
were drawn over-sized and my caption read:
"*The Monkeys take Time for Art.*"

She looked at it studiously,
sitting in the kitchen
where she read all her daily Monkeys and said,
"Oh! A *deep* Monkey."

One day I found her with her Monkey scrapbook out,
turning the pages slowly as she read,
smiling over the drawings.
Without looking up, in a quiet voice she said,
"No more Monkeys. The Monkeys are over now."

So I didn't know
I had drawn my last one. She didn't say it but
I don't think she wanted me drawing anything sad.

She made me promise never to draw Monkeys
for anyone else,
and she died a few days later.

32

I see her poised like a swimmer on the starting block
waiting for the wave,
with her arms out front, her eyes on it
over her shoulder,
and at the right moment she dives.
There's a fight for it, she's in the curl, then she's on top
straight as a board,
arms behind her back, steering with her shoulders,
head up, riding it all the way in,
grounding out at the shoreline.

She gets up laughing.
Her bathing suit is stuffed with sand,
but it still covers the chemo port on her chest
just as she made it.
She rinses out the sand and goes out for the next wave.

Sitting with her chin on her knees
arms around her legs,
she watches the water, the sandpipers chasing and fleeing
the ebb and flow of spent waves,
the gulls and terns overhead.

When there are no waves
she leaves me and walks by herself along the beach,
sometimes a mile or two
to the lifeguard station at Ventnor and back.

She knows it will be her last summer.
The beach and ocean give her peace
when she thinks of it, she says.

And when the great waves of late August came
that year
thundering and fearful,
it gave her exhilaration,
fights she could win,
and a few small triumphs.

33

I know.
It's been almost two years.
I know, I should get out,
meet people, travel,
get a part time job
or volunteer.
I know.
I should get a dog,
join a group,
take up something.
I know,
I should clear out the house,
go through her drawers,
get rid of her clothes.
I know, I know.
Leave me alone.

34

My father sometimes
used the expression
"I need that like a hole in the head."
Since he was World War Two infantry,
he must have seen enough people
with holes in their heads
to know what he was talking about.

You don't hear the expression much anymore.
My neighbor served in Viet Nam,
but when he says
"I need that like a hole in the head"
he's talking about his ex-wife—
which just goes to show
that shared experiences are not reliably
experiences shared,
and might in part explain
why I wish I didn't have to tell people
my wife died.

35

She broke off with her brother and sister
many years ago.
She had few friends.
The people she knew well
knew little of her.

I am the executor of her estate,
custodian of her belongings,
curator of her work,
and now sole arbiter
of all that will ever be known
about her.

It's a good thing she isn't here to see it.
As a general rule,
she would not want to trust me
with stuff like that.

36

I know some nights you got up
and walked around the house in the dark,
because sometimes I woke up and listened.

I watched you go around your path
in the back yard,
looking down at your feet.

I felt you far away
when you sat in the kitchen,
resting with your eyes closed,
between one book and another.

I am guessing
you were thinking about the end
while you were doing
all the things I'm doing now.

37

By her chair in the kitchen
she amassed a goodly supply
of notebooks, pencils, rulers, protractors,
squares, plastic angles, calipers and compass.

The equations she was working with
were not giving her the geometry she needed—
or something like that.

So she worked diligently away in her chair
while I sat on the floor across the room
drawing on my easel by the fireplace, being
what is commonly called company.

When I perceived little noises of success
coming from her direction,
I asked over my shoulder
"Did you get it?"
and she said "Look!"

Instead of holding up
something I would not understand,
she held out her arms for me to see
all the little hairs
standing on end.

38

If you lose some of that child capacity
for joy and exuberance,
they say you can go looking for it
with adult perseverance, and
I definitely plan to do that someday.
It's just taking my eyes so long
to get used to the dark.

39

If it were a matter of scales
and weighing one thing against another,

on one dish
I would pour the sand
of a few more years
of fellowship and food, swimming, breathing in
all the satisfactions of this world,
giving and selflessness,
loving again,

and on the other dish
I would place this single grain
of dimensionless longing.

If it were only a matter of scales
and weighing one thing against another,
there would be less to ponder in the balance.

40

I read to her in bed every night,
children's books from the library
about plucky little girls
in bad families
who used their wits to get out of tight spots.

She kept her eyes closed
and I could read and watch her face
at the same time.

It was the same face that first drew close
when she was nineteen.

It was the same face that looked up
one day when she said,
"I don't think we're going to get out of this one, Monkey."

And it was the same face
I put mine against
the only night I did not read to her.

41

The surgery left a little scar
that made it look like
she had two belly buttons.

The ham and cheese sandwiches
they sent up from the hospital kitchen
were not much bigger
than Oreo cookies. So small
we really had to wonder
how they did it.

When she could eat again
and gained back
the thirty pounds she had lost,
she was so thrilled to stand naked
between the bathroom mirrors
and show me her buttocks were back.

She made rain gear
out of an old flowered shower curtain,
and a seafaring man's hat
out of pink plastic.
In bad weather
it looked like a giant cupcake
was out walking around the yard.

Hospice called to say
it had been a year since we registered.
Because we had not called upon their services,
they were dropping us from their rolls.
We never heard of anyone
flunking out of Hospice.

There would have been some funny stories
if she had lived.

42

I wish she were here now,
making me impatient
with a long story.
I wish she were here,
trying to teach me something,
making me frustrated and angry.
I wish she were here again
when I wanted to be alone
and pushed her away.

Broken on the wheel
or stretched upon the rack
I would confess and renounce all this,
for what little good it would do.
Regret will torture to the last degree.

43

There was a sad little wooden bird,
a Pennsylvania Dutch carving
her brother gave her years ago.
It was tilted downward on short legs
with drooped wings
and head to the ground.
He looked very sad,
tethered to the earth, unaware of wing and
unknowing of the sky.

One day, she took it off the shelf,
looked at it, studied it a while,
turned it over in her hands a few times
and went to get some tools.

She removed the head and put it on the other end,
then turned the feet around, took off the wings
and reversed them to go upward.
She painted him with bright colors
and when she was done she named him

>   Free Bird!

I'm always finding things like Free Bird
around the house
and saying to myself,

Look what she did with this!

44

Sometimes we would close our books,
take off our glasses, turn out the light
and lie in bed talking
for a long time.

So I still do that,
with my eyes open, staring up
to where the ceiling should be,
seeing nothing but black
and lying so still
that after not very long
there is no sense of having arms hands feet or legs,
only a mind floating in the dark,
a little mote of consciousness
talking to another little mote on the other side of the
    universe,
waiting for her voice to come back
across the darkness of this room,
the way it always felt
when we lay awake talking,
and sometimes I can fall asleep
before I know the difference.

45

I have some of her hair
from when she cut it to shoulder length
thirty years ago.
I have one of her baby teeth
her mother saved,
rattling in a pill bottle.
They are the last earthly remains,
unless I count
the scent of her clothes, giving way
to the smell of closets and drawers,
and traces of her fingerprints
in clay figures,
and everything else that shows
the work of her hands in this house,
this reliquary,
where I live with her.

46

DAY

She rested on Sunday in the bedroom,
came out to the kitchen to work out some geometry
she would never finish,
then had to go back.
We lay on the bed for long stretches that day
in the half light of the drawn blinds,
just looking at each other,
finding little to say but I love you
back and forth.

In a few hours,
that small space between us would widen
into the great rift between the living and the dead,
but for now the bridge held,
and across it went the last messages
concerning all that had been fought over, laughed about
and lived through
for forty years.
I could feel the bridge sway over the chasm
when we closed our eyes.

NIGHT

When it got dark
she went down the basement stairs
for a last walk around her studio.

There were projects she had worked on for decades,
among them a very large armature that sometimes
wintered in the garage, titled The Old Man and the Wind,
a cloaked figure standing on a mountain, who never got
    beyond
a score of plasticine maquettes that never pleased her.

When she came up the stairs
she asked me to dismantle it
but otherwise took only the smallest notice of me,
and there was nothing on her face
but the determination it took to get up the steps
and last another hour.

She was so weak I had to help her in the shower
and into a nightgown.
Then, standing on her own,
straight as she always stood,
she took off her wedding band and engagement ring
and put them in a little box.

She got into bed and asked me
to bring in what she had to drink
and the instructions we had gone over
with the pharmacist.

I came back from the kitchen
with the first glass
and sat beside her on the bed.
She said she couldn't look at me or talk or listen to
    anything I said.
She had to focus on drinking three glasses of poison,
and wait thirty minutes between each, when, for the
    last week,
she had not been able to hold down even ice chips.

She said if she threw up
she would drink it back from the bowl
and she told me what to do if it didn't work.
She made me promise.
There was no going back.

The first glass went down and the second,
and she fought to hold them through the intervals.
Getting ready for the third, she said,
"I didn't think anything could taste so bad."

She gagged on the third, threw up, drank the last of the glass
and was reaching for the bowl
when she turned a startled face to me,
as if she had suddenly looked down and found herself
in mid air at a great height
or across a deep chasm
from where I was.

Then her eyes closed
and she sank back to the pillow.
Her heart beat and she breathed a minute or two longer
and then everything stopped.

Her face was in perfect calm
lovely and remote
as though it had no further need
of fight or determination
and had decided
living was easier that way.

I lay beside her through the night
with part of me thinking she might wake up
and be all right again.

47

Forgive me,
but I do not understand
why people want to live so long
after losing what they could not live without.

Now here I am
doing it too.
Forgive me.

48

Thinking back now, how casually
without any thought to it
we kissed, embraced,
tossed off I love you
so many times a day
for forty years
that neither of us remembered
the first time for each one
and no dates were ever recorded.

There must have been
a last time for each of them too,
but I failed to notice
and there is no one left to ask.

49

July 12.
Her birthday.
I remembered this time.
No one else has,
because she is in the process
of being forgotten.

She has had two null and void birthdays
since her last one living,
when she turned sixty.
It was one of those they call a milestone,
notable for having made it at all.

We were at the beach that day
and she was happily riding her waves.

I am there now, in the same place
and it looks like the same people are here,
and the world has gone on just fine
forgetting those gone on,
and I'm thinking why not
I might as well
sneak off with her.

50

That year
some nice parts of it
came down to just the two of us
living with each other the way we did,
without the outside world,
as if we had made a jump to advanced age,
and taken up the quiet life
of books and our own work.

But as it was,
she was dying young
and I was there to watch.

51

By the time her last day came
I think I saw in her face
the realization
that her life had been unhappy.

She wouldn't blame anyone
or cry for herself
or leave me with the thought,
but I knew.

We had a long life together.
I should have attended to it.
I could have done something
before she went spending
all that time
on me.

52

I can make little changes
to suit myself,
I can put the forks
where the spoons always were.
But how can I have another life
without believing she's gone.

53

We put our hands together
and compared fingers,
feet to compare toes
and legs up in the air
to look at our kneecaps side by side.

Suffering in the comparison
are my ordinary fingers,
toes I have never found a use for,
and square blocky knees.

Her fingers were long and slender,
so were her toes,
and they were just as smart as her fingers because
whenever she needed an extra hand,
she just took off a shoe.

Her kneecaps were
sublime little caps.
But one was unruly,
expressing its discontent with straight lines
by dislocating from time to time.
In great pain
she would stretch the leg out,
take a deep breath, grimace, and whack it back in line
with a sharp blow of her hand.

Sometimes it took more than one hit
but she was a pretty tough cookie.

Setting aside the trick knee,
between her inventive mind
and the skills
of her fingers and toes,
she set out to do great things,
and might have,
but what survives in this world?
ordinary fingers like mine,
blocky kneecaps,
and toes that only know
how to poke holes in socks.

54 DRIVING HOME

From one day to the next
the sun is in a long low slant
over the pine barrens
foretelling the end of summer.

Going west from the shore
passing through little towns
in long silences
looking sideways out the window
at nothing
but the old familiar road,
and our faces reflecting back in the glass
our upended dreams
time lost
and sorrows of the absent.
We recognized loneliness
without having to ask.

When we get home
we just hold each other a little longer than usual,
turn on some lights,
make dinner,
and everything is fine again.

55

In quiet moments
seeking the deeply profound in simple things,
as sometimes we did,
we put our hands together
with our wedding bands touching,
thinking on what they signified,
half expecting
to see them link spontaneously
by the loving force between us.

So I will go on wearing mine
until my last night.
Then I will remove it myself as she did
and place it with hers before I go.

Maybe they will be kept together,
grace the hands of others
and outlive other loves.

What a sad job to have
for more than one lifetime.

56 A LITTLE HISTORY

One day, she packed samples of her work into a suitcase
    on wheels
and went to the Walnut Street Theater in Philadelphia.
They weren't looking for help
but she came home with a job in the costume shop.

Many years before, at sixteen, she worked at Dunkin' Donuts
From 4 am until just in time to catch a bus at 8
to Alternative School in the city.

At seventeen she was apprenticed to a German bookbinder
out in the woods of Pennsylvania, doing restorations
    for museums.
She lived in the attic and ate German food.
When the master saw what she could do,
he jumped way ahead and taught her gold leaf.

She joined me at nineteen. She was taking a bus every day
to college in North Jersey. I got her a little car. She got a
    driver's license.
Then it was Rutgers Camden, parking under the
    Ben Franklin Bridge.
On graduation day, I was in another part of town,
    joining hands
with strangers at the appointed hour
for Hands Across America

so I missed it. None of her family came either. She might
  have been
the only one thoughtful enough to be proud of her.

She got a job fixing sewing machines. She got another one
making curtains half the size of a football field
for the Philadelphia Convention Center.

She made arms and hands in a prosthetics lab. She cooked
for Whole Foods, she was taken on by Raymond James
to learn the trade and take the Series Seven.

She sewed bridal and the owner wanted her to take over
  the shop.
She commuted to New York three days a week,
working for a designer, which entailed a commission
for the Clinton White House.

She taught sewing, construction, and design in adult night
  school,
tutored Drexel fashion students,
taught everyone from grandmothers to children,
sold her own line of casual wear
at the Jersey shore, made leather outfits for
gay biker couples, Santa Claus suits for Santa Clauses,
and custom clothing for the disabled and wheelchair bound.

She went to a packaging manufacturer
to ask if they needed a CAD/CAM operator.
It was the only job she didn't get, because they were closing.
She hurried home to buy stock
in the company that was buying them out.

Her last twelve years was with the Seward Johnson Atelier,
making clothing for sculptures destined for resin and
    bronze.
By the time she fell sick and came home
there were not many people in the world who did what
    she did
or knew what she knew.

From an early age
she was beset with low blood pressure,
digestive problems, and allergies
that gave her a life-long fear she wouldn't be able to work.
So work was the mountain,
and every day
the strength of her will the climber.

It was a life of many accomplishments,
but she died before she ever saw it that way.

57

I followed her
through many doors.
I followed her into the ocean
wading out to catch waves.
But when we walked together,
she was always on my left.
When we sat down and when we slept,
or came to a new place,
feeling her on my left
was a way of knowing
where I was.

58

The path in the backyard is covering over
with grass that never knew her,
but remembered how to grow
when she was gone.
The generation of squirrels she talked to
has returned to the earth,
and the birds and butterflies that fluttered behind her
seem to have followed her away.

Haikus composed in her head as she walked the path
are in little notebooks I cannot bear to look for.
She hurried inside to write them down every night
while I dug dirt from the treads of her boots,
and shook the rain or snow off the blue cloak and hat
    she made.

The path is a long oval, from the backyard
down to a ravine and creek bed
before the rise of the railroad tracks.

At night I would stand outside
on the high back porch
and wait for her to come into the lights of the house,
make the turn,
and disappear again into the dark.

What I wouldn't give
to be back there waiting
to untie laces, send her inside and
dig dirt out of treads
while boots are still warm from her feet.

59

When love goes away
it takes everything with it.
When love goes away
you know
how much it did for you.
When love goes away
it leaves a body
that goes on waking and sleeping,
hungering and eating,
and you can stay dead on your feet
a long time
when love goes away.

60

Whenever there were things
she wanted to forget,
she didn't allow herself
too much time up in the clouds
or let her thoughts stray
or go too deep.

I am finding a need for that now,
as I remember how she looked
when she did it for herself,
how her eyes opened wide and narrowed down,
taking in everything around her.

I could tell she was calculating an angle,
judging a distance,
following a movement,
evaluating a shape,
or noting lines of light and shadow.

And then she turned all the information of her eyes
over to her hands,
and what came out of it in clay,
charcoal, paint or chalk
never showed a trace
of what she was trying to forget.

61

It took me a while, but I figured out
we did say goodbye after all.
I just didn't know it at the time.

I was sent out on a hunt
for Pennsylvania Dutch Birch Beer
because it brought back memories of Cape May
when she was a girl,
when it was where wealthy families from all over
sent their alcoholics, misfits and non-conformists.

She told stories about Old Man Joe,
a cranky eccentric millionaire
beach bum and great pal,
in self-exile from his beachfront Victorian mansion
and flock of unmarried sisters;
Olga, the Russian émigré, constant companion
and dearest mother to her;
Pete, the handy-man, shell-shocked war veteran,
and others I don't remember now.

I found Pennsylvania Dutch Birch Beer in early September.
By then, she could only take sips,
but it was enough to bring back memories of all those people,
the ocean, the rock jetties, the docks, seagulls, and smells
    she had grown up with
of seaweed, fish, and tar.

In the afternoon of her last day, she lay down in the cool
    dark of the bedroom
resting for what she had to do that night.
She asked me to bring her a glass of Birch Beer
and a glass for myself.

We sat on the bed, holding our little Coke-bottle glasses
and she laughed because
hers only had a thimble full,
which was all she could take.

She smiled a big smile and clicked her glass against mine.
She said, "I love you so much"
as if we were just at the beginning,
or made love for the first time,
or just moved into the house—
as if we had just succeeded at something.

A few months passed
and thinking over that afternoon again,
it came to me, that as far back as I remember,
we never clicked our glasses together until then.

I like to think
we saved it for goodbye.

62

The first years we took up with each other,
there were ashtrays in the bedroom
and she stayed up all night reading.
In those days
I came home to the trash
overflowing with empty beer cans.
She wasn't sure
what she was going to do.

But before long,
the house filled up with what she learned,
what she made, ideas she had.

Little robots she built walked around the house,
orphan sewing machines off the street
gathered here, with
every known kitchen appliance, old and new,
stacks of annual reports and market projections,
bags of black walnuts she gathered for ink, tools of diverse
trades, bins of cardboard, vats of paper mache,
buckets of clay and plaster.

Strings of abstract origami hung from the attic rafters
over computers she cobbled together,
freestanding chalkboards with equations and geometry,
and everywhere books from library book sales.

Books in every corner,
piles of books by the bed,
Chinese philosophy, mathematics, nutrition,
sewing, engineering, architecture,
a wall of cookbooks,
walls of art books,
computer programing, knots,
how to make shoes, finance, electronics
and always more.
Her mind never rested.

I didn't have much to do with it.
There were probably people in the Renaissance
who didn't know what was going on either.
I just helped her carry the books in.

63

She gave me names of people to call
after she was gone,
but she was such a master of spatial dimension
you'd never know
that truckloads of fabric, machines, and tools
were taken out of this house.

It stopped when I got down
to what I knew how to use,
what I wanted around me
and what I knew she loved.

I will leave what remains
for others after me
and for now,
I will live with the dust and echoes
that are taking her place.
Then someone else will live here.

64

For months we sat
in medical office waiting rooms,
walked through grand foyers of hospitals
laid out like airport terminals.
We circled around parking lots
looking for the MRI building, the CAT scan facility,
took the steps down to X-ray,
waited outside the Ultrasound room.

I sat with her and held her purse in my lap.
She was a mystery to everyone,
so we made the rounds again
with every new doctor
as she weakened every day.

Then a blind stab at surgery
just before she starved to death,
and we got lucky.
Then the infusion center,
where the other kind of luck came back.

The last one on our dance card
was the oncologist, who told us
it was terminal.
He had always been honest
so she asked me for a pen
and one of the little notebooks

from her purse.
She asked him,
"How long do I have?"
"How will I die?"
There was not much to write down.

Walking out the doors of medical
for the last time, we felt like kids
getting out on the last day of school,
when summer seems to stretch forever.

65

PART ONE: FITS AND STARTS

It might be safe to say that in art
she looked for what the medium wanted to express.

I would point to her backyard installation
after a storm,
of a human figure made of fallen tree limbs,
to experiments in bamboo
lashed with wisteria vine,
also to haunting little figures in tree bark
standing on slate, looking up
with imploring hickory nut faces,
and to swiftly executed Chinese goldfish and elephant
    heads
shaped with no time to spare
from leftover plaster.

Pursuing any idea,
she made tiny origami Oxford shirts
the size of postage stamps,
a miniature upholstered couch
a full scale Van Gogh bed
modeled after the painting,
an aerial performance of copper wire figures
hanging from the ceiling,
and from there, experiments in lighting
and stage set design.

PART TWO: COLLABORATION

When she got too weak to wrestle around bags of plaster,
she taught me mold making
and I cast a few of her pieces,
with mixed success and a few lost ears and noses.

She thought I might someday conceptualize her aesthetic
or vision, if that were possible,
and write something down for her
if she ever made it to the art world.

With that in mind, I named some pieces—
a long-legged girl in a billowing dress
built with armature wire, brown paper and orange netting
that looked very Paris runway—
Pipi Guggenheim.
She liked that one, and it sustained her long desire
that we would make things together.

Then I arranged a grouping of her paper mache heads
in a woven basket and titled it—
"Bastille Day,"
which slightly dismayed her.

She wanted our art to be uplifting.

PART THREE: TWO YEARS LATER

This afternoon I saw a young fly
touching down on a warm board of the porch
and thought how unfortunate for him
to come out in January. He didn't know.
He'll die tonight from the cold.

I wonder what she could have done
with thirty more years,
but thoughts like that
have nowhere to go in winter.

66

The world without her
is really just me
without her,
going on in our little house,
in the little world
we made for ourselves,
the year and a half
we knew she was going to die.

Now I wait here
pending repatriation
to the big world,
that for our year away,
never considered us a great loss.

67 WHY I HAVE NO PLANS TO VISIT NATIONAL PARKS

Our backyard
had plenty of nature.
We lived in it, looked out the windows at it
and I can still walk the path
she made with her feet through it.

The river
where we first went to talk.
I can go there,
sit on the high quay
watch the barges and Pennsylvania shore
and remember us young.

I can go to the beach
to the same place
she rode her waves, and I can look out to sea
where my ashes will be with hers.

What business do I have with the Grand Canyon?
I would only ask myself
What am I doing here?
I liked the nature we had back home.

So if you don't mind,
I'll stick with my shrinking habitat.

Like a barn owl.

68

She loved little change purses
and always came up with correct change
from one of those vintage black snaps,
or an art deco she made with Velcro closure
or a Chinese silk she sewed
with fold-over flap.

She tried not to notice impatient people
standing in line behind us,
watching as she counted out pennies,
looking like a little girl
and an old lady
at the same time.

God, I loved her.

69

At low tide
the graveyard of her sunken ships
appeared here and there out of the water

wrecks
sent to the bottom
by reef and storm
iceberg
torpedo and rust

vessels of childhood and dream
pretty little skiffs
built and varnished so carefully by
small hands

and there tangles of rigging
strung between broken masts

there too the ironclads and dreadnoughts
lie on their sides in the sand forever
and go back under returning tide

for her memory was deeper
than current could ever carry away.

70

She learned how to do
a great many things.
But childhood pulled tight
a hard knot inside
she never could untie.

71

Two years.
I should be getting over it
but I'm going the other way
and what I'm getting over
is wanting to get over it.

If it had gone the other way,
maybe she would have found a direction
to go without asking
what is one without the other, but maybe not
and I try to be grateful,
for her sake I'm taking the place
she never wanted
in what we always thought would happen.

But just the same,
living is beginning to hurt
badly enough
to call it sacrifice.

72

There seems to be nothing here
but what she left behind,
and nothing in the air
but remembering.

But I cannot make her
out of words,
I cannot draw her face from memory,
or tell a hundredth part of what she was alive.

I cannot even say
what I was then—
for all this remembering.

73

She was pretty simple
but no one was any good
at figuring that out.

It wasn't just that she faced
square to the world, she did it
without religion, without spirituality,
self-delusion or fantasy.

It was obvious to her
that there was only one life
and she was perfectly clear
on the responsibility it conferred.

She believed in the individual,
and good behavior.
She believed in loving one person best,
loyalty, devotion to duty, defending the weak,
and for most of that
she thanked Dr. Seuss for *Horton Hears a Who!*
which she read as a child
and which she forever took to be
the first and last word in morality.

That was pretty much my girl.
So naturally
people completely baffled her.

74

Among other things
of the dearest sort,
the bedroom was a refuge.
At night
we closed the blinds
pulled up the drawbridge
shut out the little savageries of the day,
and swept contentions between us
under the dark.

We slept on our own sides of the bed
or together in the middle,
but I usually found one spot
and stayed there until morning,
while throughout the night,
she was all over, shifting, turning
pushing and pulling refuge
for all it was worth.

75   PURELY SPECULATION

All she ever wanted
was her mother's love
a house to live in
that would not burn down
or get taken away,
a boy to play with,
work to do and a world of things to learn,

and for these in the striving
she was as bright and trusting
as a child.

But she never won
her mother's love,
and in some measure
for all her efforts,
it doomed the rest.

76

For every joyous moment
I see just as readily
her face disappearing
under the black zipper of the body bag
that dark morning,
for every time she turned to kiss me
I see her throwing up over the toilet
her in the snow,
her at the beach,
her lying dead beside me
like before and after pictures
as seen from after
memory brings up
more than you would ever bargain for
dim the lights
sit back, put out a hand
to the empty chair
and watch
God help us grieving.

77

Unless I am going to be living
on the wild coast of Ireland
in a rugged Hogarthian cottage writing a novel,
becoming a fully actualized alone-person
seems to me
neither an enviable state of being,
nor a worthwhile aspiration.

In the immediate neighborhood here,
there are no fewer than eleven such households,
and I give them credit
for their positive attitudes
and cheery dispositions.
Not one of them seems likely
to put a gun to his or her head
anytime soon.

But this is a life I will never love.
I cannot forget that one person
can make all the difference in the world,
and Lisa Ann Holland Chang was a person
and a half.

Thank you for loving me.

eric

ABOUT THE AUTHOR

Eric B. Miller grew up in southern New Jersey. He holds a master's degree in English and pursued writing while working on farms in Virginia, Maryland, and Belgium. He spent twenty years in the business world back in New Jersey, then eighteen years in the American Red Cross, and recently began writing again. He is the author of *Hula Girls*, a novel.

www.ingramcontent.com/pod-product-compliance
Lightning Source LLC
LaVergne TN
LVHW041335080426
835512LV00006B/461